OOR WULLIE

*Selected from
'The Sunday Post'
and 'Oor Wullie' Books.*

D. C. THOMSON & Co., Ltd., GLASGOW : LONDON : DUNDEE

45p

A

A GREAT SPORT!

O OR Wullie likes the fishin'—
For fun it beats the lot.
But there's one thing that's certain—
He'll catch it if HE'S caught!

The game o' tennis that he plays
Is great—ye canna whack it!
He wields Ma's brand-new frying pan—
It makes a bonny 'racket'!

No whistlin' refs are there to watch
Oor Wullie's fitba' game.
But guess who's there wi' wee black book
To jot doon oor star's name!

Oor Wullie dresses for the part
When on the golfin' tees—
The only lad you'll ever see
In plus-four dungarees!

In summer, there's the cricket—
He's up to all his tricks.
Trust Oor Wullie to find out
A new way to hit 'six'!

So there you have it, five great sports,
With rod and bat and ball,
As played by your own Wullie—
THE BEST SPORT OF THEM ALL!

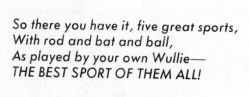

Wull's chased and soaked, but well contented—
With the proverb HE invented!

Who's this stranger striding in—

Shining like a brand new pin?

Here comes Tex with gun and rope—

He thinks he's rough and tough—some hope!

Wullie's smart! See what he's got—

A smashing 'portable' guess-what!

What's this? Oor Wullie scared to fight?

Ah, there's good reason for his flight!

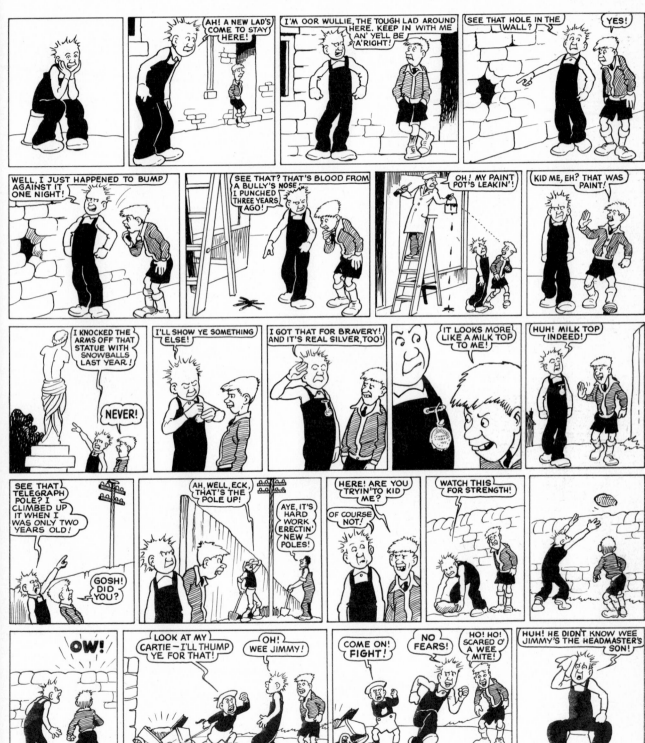

All this din gives folk a pain—

No wonder they stop Wullie's playin'!

Oor Wullie's feeling really grim—

All his jokes backfire on him!

Wull finds a worm, as you'll see—
Not underground—but up a tree!

"Cissie Wullie!" That's the shout—

But when Miss Lamb hits back—look out!

This lad's useless, so Wull thinks—
Till he gets up to some HIGH jinks!

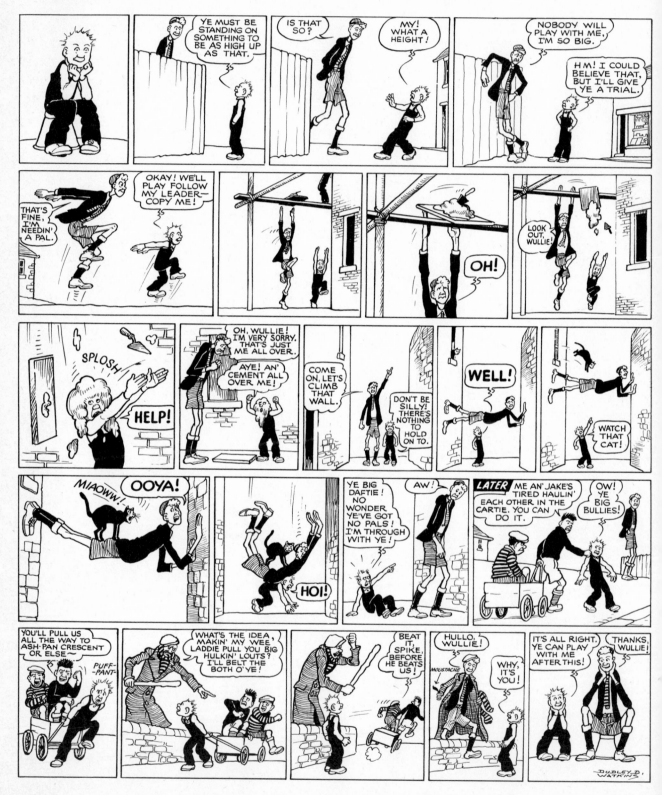

Wullie's got a strange disguise—

But just when things look black—surprise!

THIS DICK WHITTINGTON OUTFIT MIGHT WIN ME A PRIZE AT THE FANCY DRESS PARTY!

DICK WHITTINGTON AND HIS CAT, EH? OH, YOU'LL WIN FIRST PRIZE, WULLIE.

COME BACK, YE SILLY CAT.

YE'VE RUINED MY ACT! DICK WHITTINGTON'S NO USE WITHOOT A CAT!

I'LL NEED TO GO AS SOMETHING ELSE, NOW!

AH, A BOY WI' A PATCH OVER HIS EYE.
AND DON'T YOU TAKE IT OFF, JAMIE!

ACH! I'M NO' GOIN' ABOOT WI' THAT ON!
H'M! THAT GIES ME AN IDEA!

HULLO, WULLIE! PLAYIN' AT PIRATES?
YES, I'M GOIN' TO A FANCY DRESS PARTY!

GIVE ME THAT PATCH—IT'S JAMIE'S! HE NEEDS IT FOR HIS SORE EYE!
AW!

THAT'S SPOILT MY PIRATE GET-UP.
ACH, NOW MY HAT'S AWA'!

HELP! I DIDN'T SEE THE WATER!

NOW I'M SOAKED!
SHIVER!
WAIT, WULLIE—I'LL GIVE YE A COAT O' MY DAUGHTER'S TO KEEP YE WARM.

IT'S A BIT TIGHT AN' LONG—BUT IT'LL DO.
AW, THANKS.

H'M! I'VE AN IDEA!

HULLO, WULLIE! SO YE'RE GOIN' TO THAT FANCY DRESS PARTY AS NAPOLEON!
AYE, PAW. I AM THAT!

ON A BIT
MY LUCK'S IN AGAIN.
HEY! YE'RE ON MY NEW-LAID TAR!

WAIT TILL I GET A HOLD O' YE!

I CANNA GO BACK FOR MY HAT—THAT MAN LOOKS AWFY BAD-TEMPERED.

I'VE LOST MY HAT NOW. I'LL SIT DOON HERE AN' THINK WHIT I'M TO DO NEXT.

A GOOD SPOT TO DUMP MY SOOT.

AYE, WULLIE SHOULD WIN A PRIZE FOR THAT DICK WHITTINGTON RIG-OUT!
PIRATE, YE MEAN!
NO, NO—NAPOLEON!
CHILDREN'S FANCY DRESS PARTY PRIZE FOR BEST COSTUME

WULLIE! WHERE'S YER FANCY DRESS COSTUME? YE'RE JUST SOLID BLACK! YE DIDN'T GET A PRIZE FOR THAT SURELY?
OH, AYE! FIRST PRIZE—FOR GOIN' AS A STICK OF LICORICE!
DRESS NOT DRESS BOY PRIZE BEST UME

DUDLEY D. WATKINS

Some funny things sure come to pass—
When Wullie's asked to polish brass!

Wull's out of luck! He goes too far—
In his one-wheeled 'motor car'!

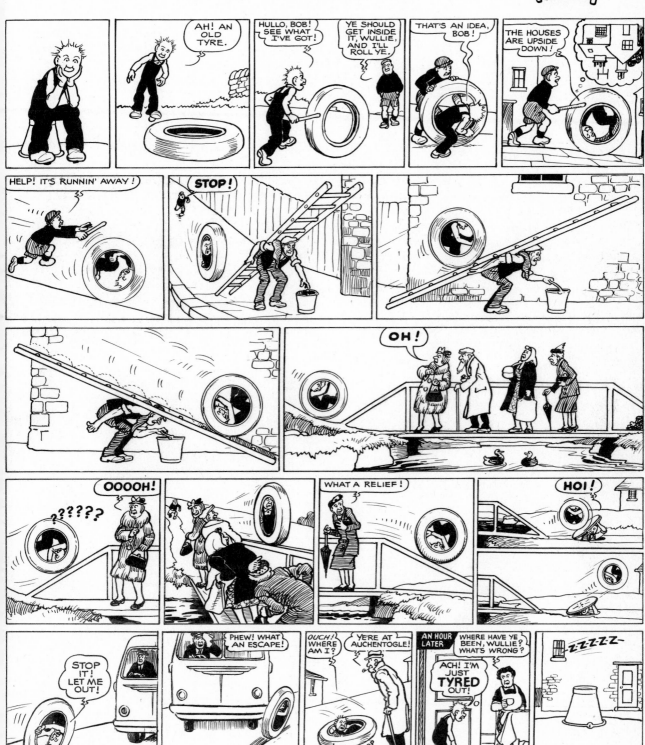

It's not 'eggs'-actly funny when—

Oor Wullie has to catch a hen!

LOOK! THERE'S A HEN RUNNIN' OOT O' THAT BUT AN' BEN.

COME BACK, YE WEE HEN!

CLUCK, CLUCK!

SHE'S AYE RUNNIN' AWA'. WHERE DID SHE GO? I'LL GET HER FOR YE, WIFIE!

COME HERE, YE WEE MADAM!

GOT YE~ NO~ ESCAPED!

I'LL NEED TO BE CRAFTY~ THERE'S A WORM!

COME ON, HENNIE. HERE'S A TREAT FOR YE.

HELP~ THAT CROW PINCHED IT~

CLUCK! CLUCK!

LATER. OH! THAT DOG~ RUNNIN' STRAIGHT AT THE HEN!

WHIT A SHAME~ I CANNA LOOK!

GOOD DOG. GIVE ME THE BALL.

ACH! IT WISNA RUNNIN' AT THE WEE HEN EFTER A'!

I'LL GET HER THIS TIME. SHE'S RIGHT AT THE EDGE O' THE WATER!

GOT HER~ NO!

THE WEE RASCAL'S JUMPED INTO THE BOAT~ I CAN HARDLY REACH IT.

HELP! I'M NEARLY IN THE WATER.

WELL, O' A' THE COOL CHEEK! SHE TAK'S ME FOR A BRIDGE!

HELP! I'M DROONIN'!

CLUCK-CLUCK!

ACH! I'M SOAKED! TO POT WI' THIS! I'M AWA' HAME.

LOOK! IT'S SITTIN' ON A BUCKET LIKE I DO.

TUCK-TUCK-TUCK~

GOT YE THIS TIME!

HERE'S YER HEN, WIFIE, AN' SHE'S LAID AN EGG!

AN' I GOT THE EGG!

HAPPY EASTER!

TAP-TAP

DUDLEY D. WATKINS

Gives Cousin George big shocks!

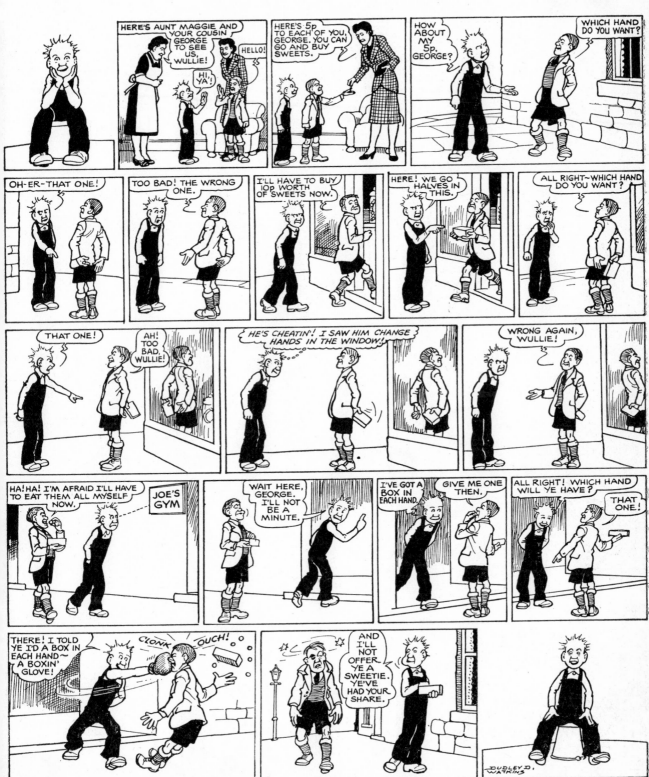

B

Oh, what a battle—

With Farmer Wilson's cattle!

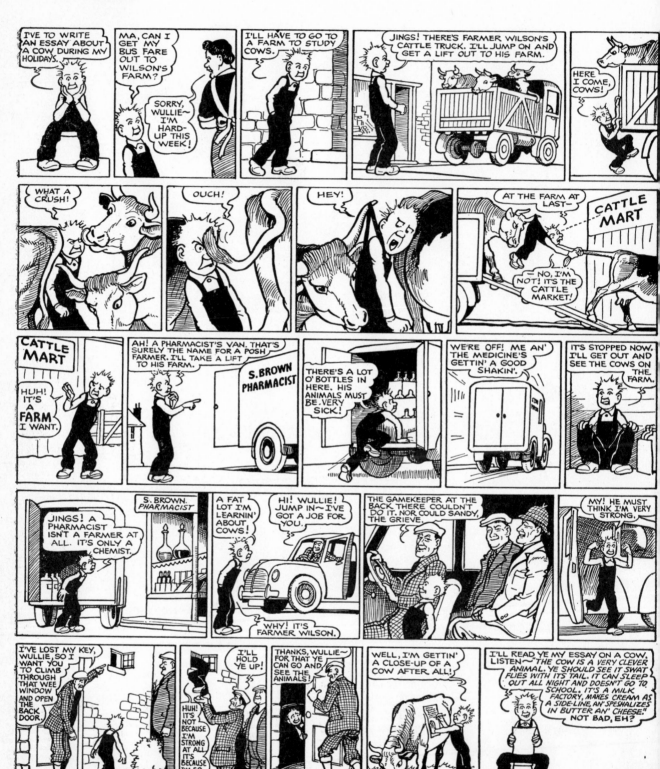

Parp! Honk! Hoot! Oor Wullie's fated—
To have his tooter confiscated!

Three baked apples on a plate—

It's Wullie's favourite dish—but wait . . .!

What a tee-hee—

At Ma's sewing bee!

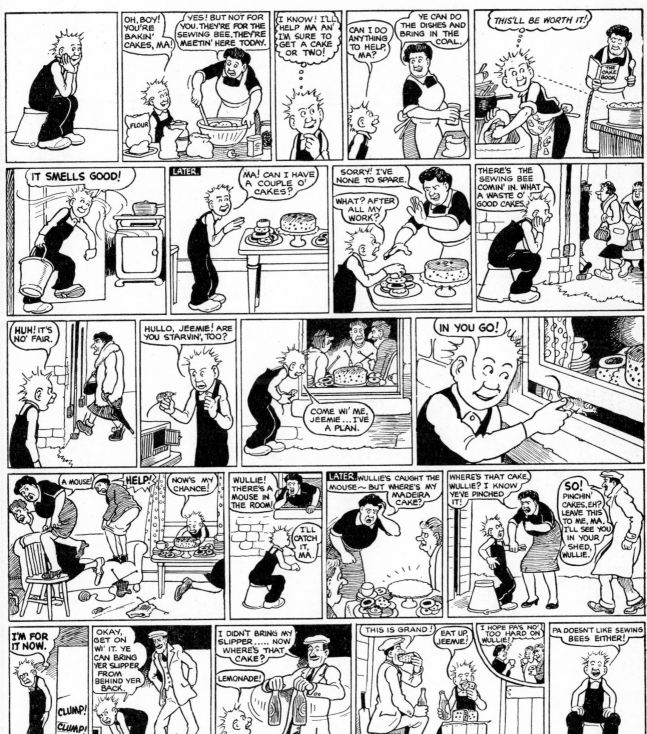

Oor Wullie's pals are shocked, you bet—

When Wullie is the teacher's pet!

'Butter fingers' is his name—

But watch him at this football game!

Wullie's broke, but he's no fool—

See his smashing driving school!

Why is Pa going through the town—

With one black boot and one that's brown?

Some lads get the strap with ease—

Oor Wullie WANTS it, if you please!

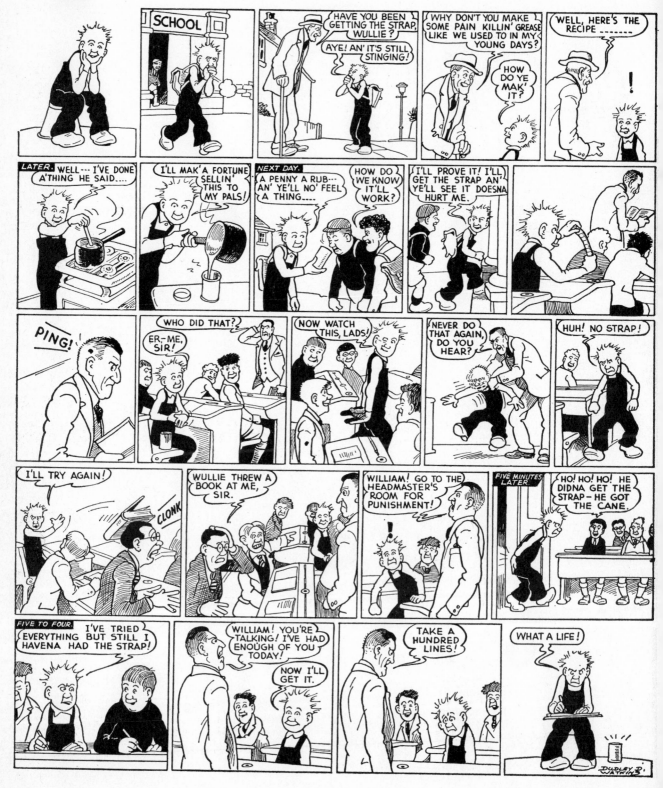

Wullie's shocked when he meets Sandy—

But everything turns out just dandy!

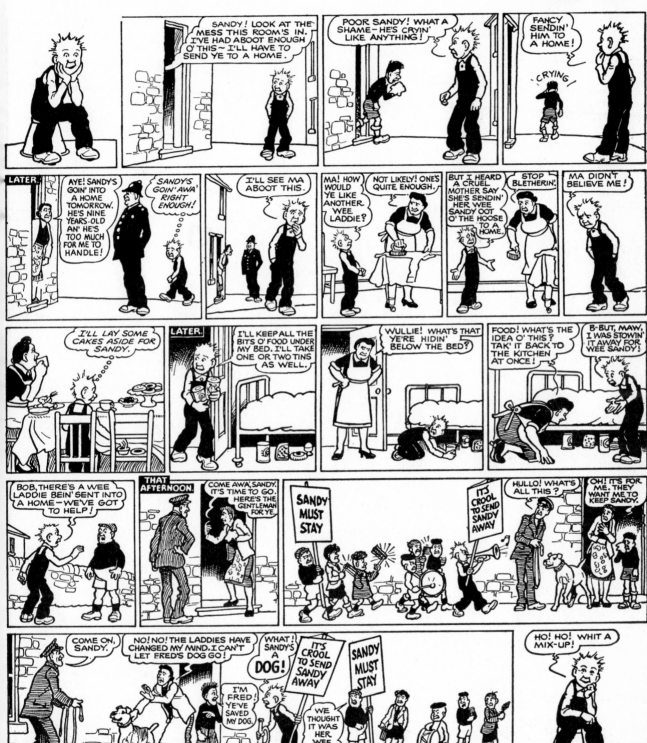

Wull's bucket's bending like elastic—

But it's not magic—it's just p_a_t_c!

All Wullie's plans come to a stop—

Until he makes a crafty swop!

Who's the new boss? That's the question—

And Wullie's last in their selection!

Oor Wullie's smart, and everyone'll—

Laugh at his tricks with a funnel!

Two chums think they'll see Wull get tanned—

But things don't work out as they planned!

Two wee laddies, keeping quiet?—

When they try, it's like a riot!

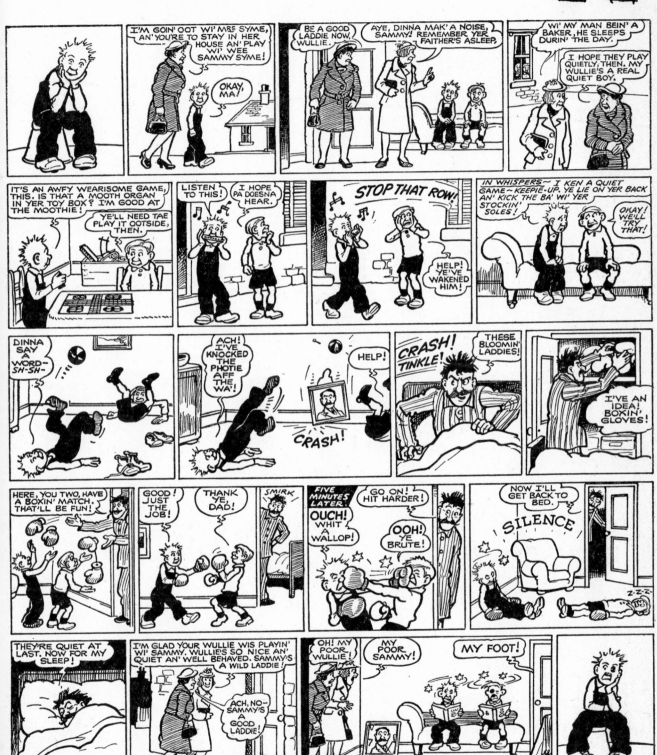

Oor Wullie knows the very thing—

To get old Murdoch on a string!

The treasure trove Wull's going to find—

Is not quite what he had in mind!

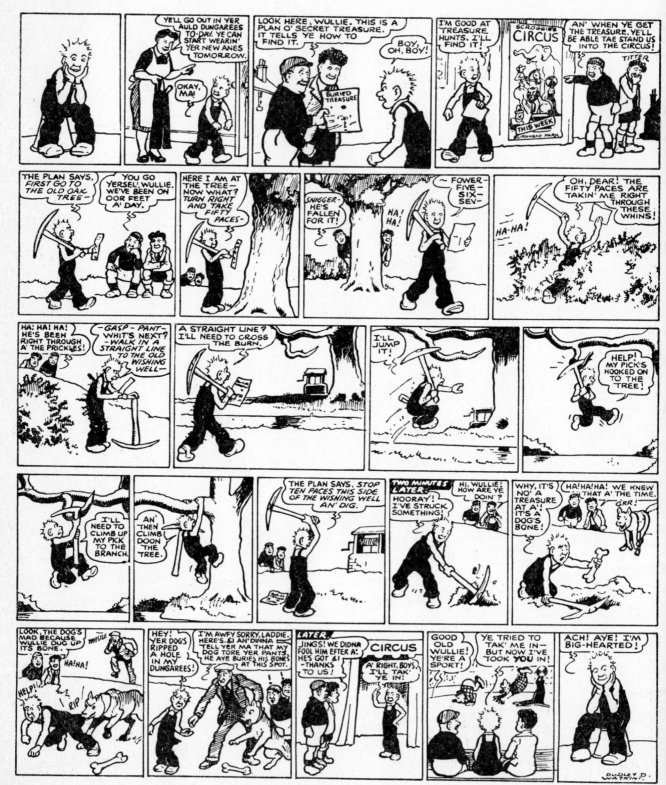

Wullie sure was sold a pup—

Eck got his story 'jumbled' up!

Here's Wullie and Wee Danny Dunn—

Bent on mischief, just for fun!

Starting handle? Megaphone?—

See Oor Wullie's gramophone!

Barber Wullie ends up yelping—

His scalping earns him a skelping!

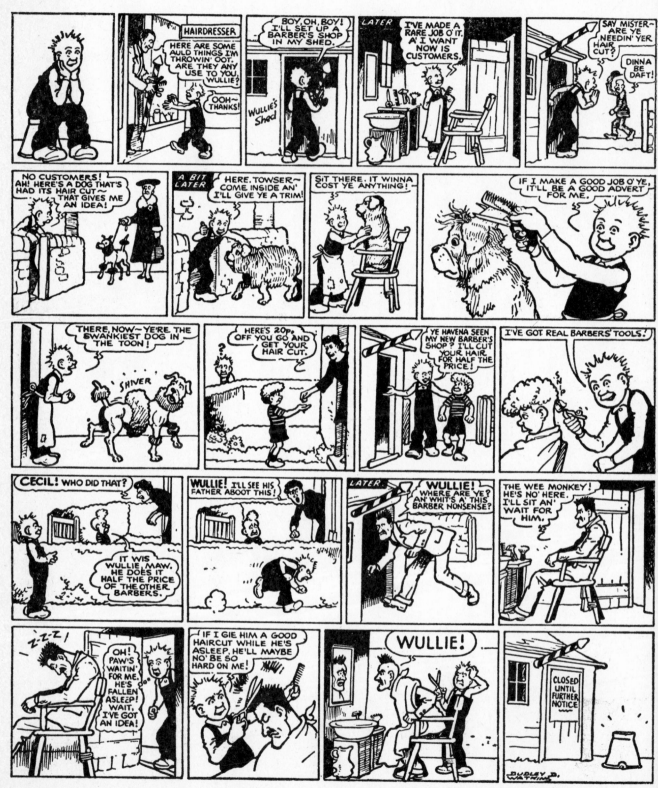

Wullie's bonny budgie's dumb—

And that's sure lucky for his chum!

Wull boards a ship, and then he braves—

A life aboard the harbour waves!

Luck's not with oor fly wee buddy—

He ends up dusty, black and muddy!

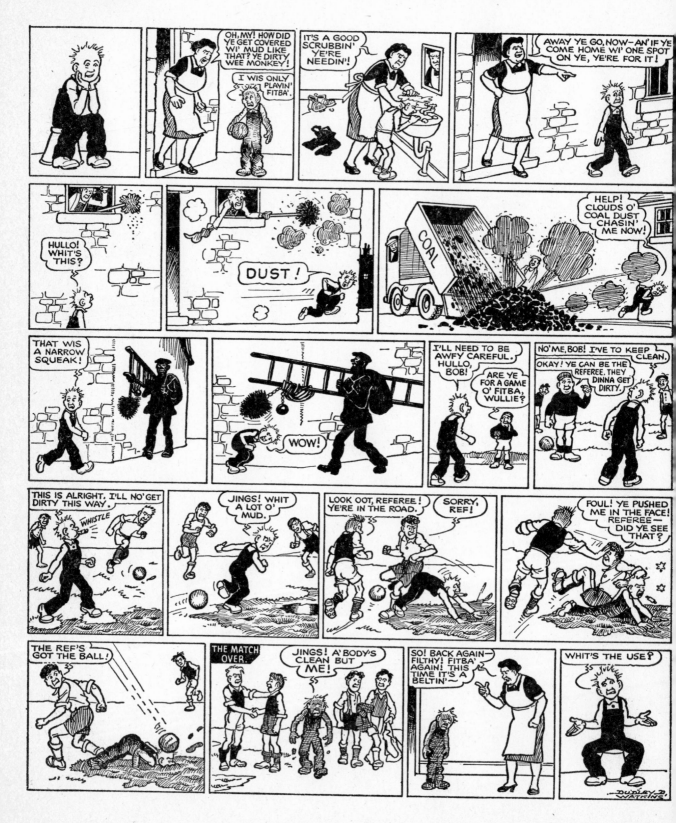

Gloves for Wullie? He's too tough—

He swops them for some other stuff!

A punch on the nose, a sock in the eye—

But Wullie and Bob just stand there. Why—?

Wull's car goes at real high speeds—
Dog biscuits are the fuel it needs!

Push a button, pull a string—

And Wullie's tent does everything.

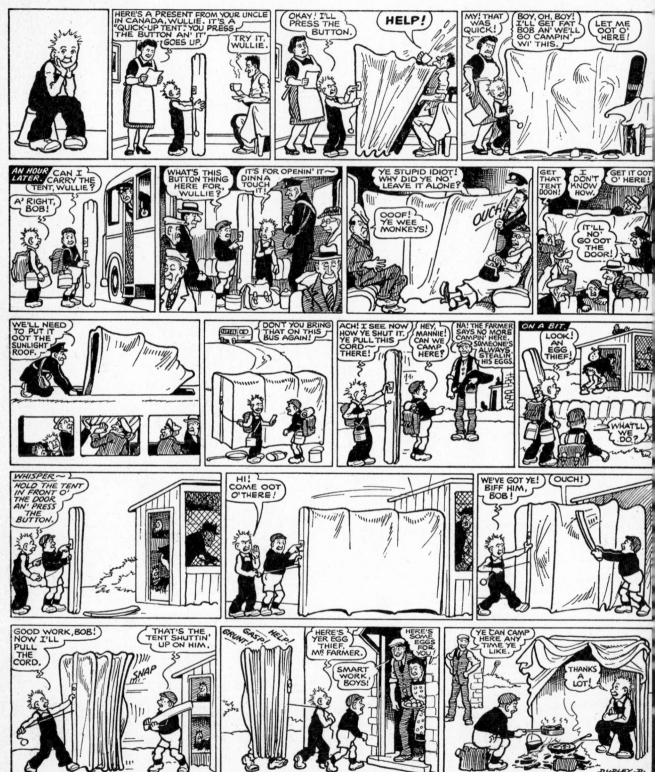

Things don't work out very well—

When Wullie does a 'William Tell'!

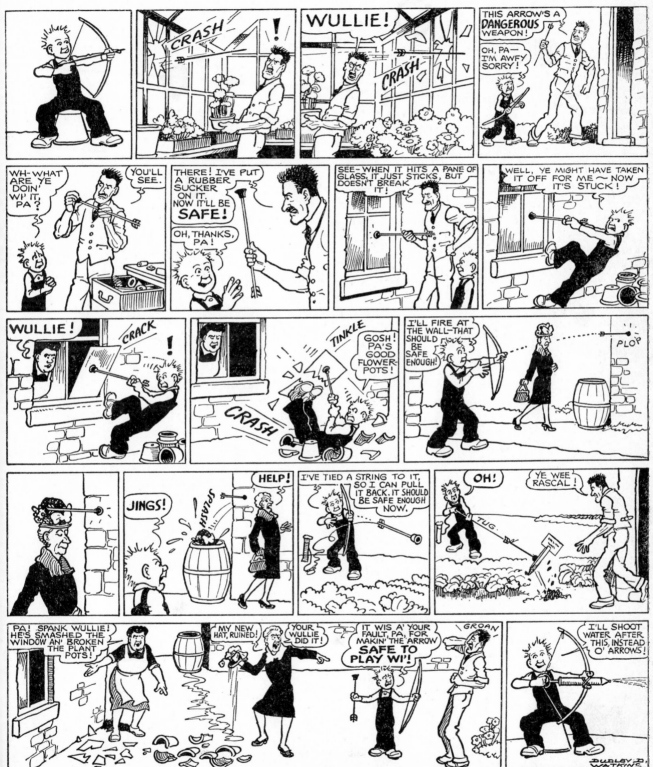

Refrigerator—comfy seat—

Oor Wullie's bucket's hard to beat!

He's blamed for this, he's blamed for that—

Oor Wullie's always on the mat!

What's this? Wull mustn't say a word—
For three long hours? THAT'S just absurd!

No donkey rides, no seaside sand—
But Wullie's day trip turns out grand!

Wullie's reward for all his hiking—

Is not exactly to his liking!

Though gravity makes apples fall—

For quick results just use a ball!

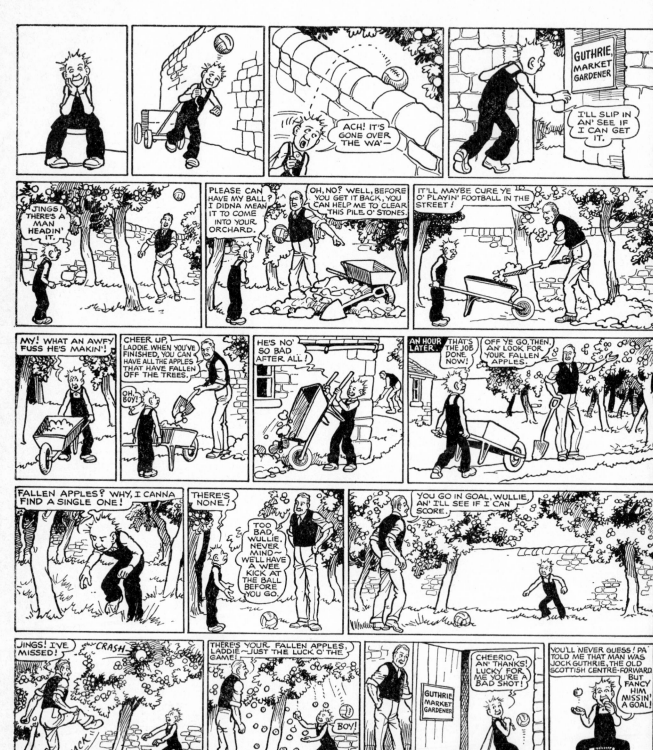

Oor Wullie dishes out big shocks—

With five spare sets of curly locks!

Wull's sure he's lost his big balloon—

Until at long last he sits doon!

Temptation sends Oor Wullie batty—

When he goes 'hunting' with his catty!

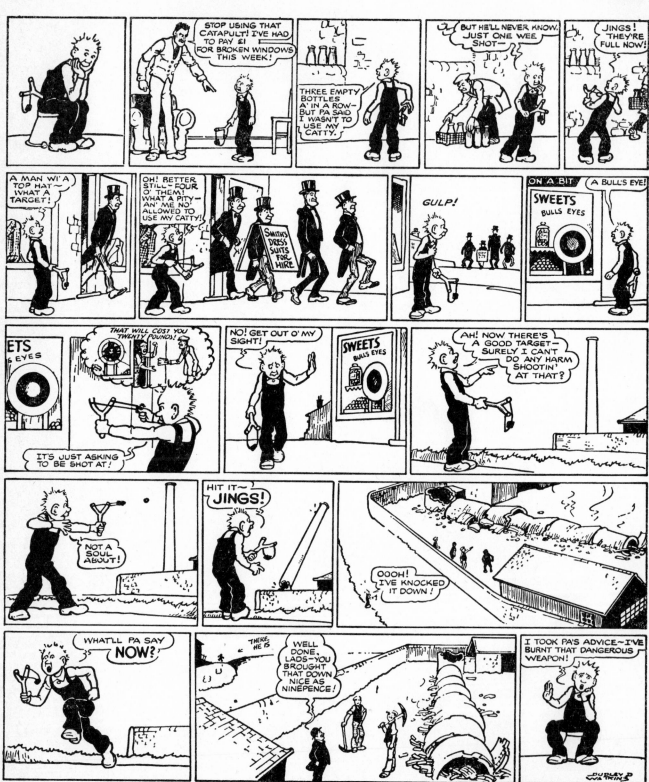

This sweetie looks a real humdinger—

When Wullie puts it through the wringer!

See how Wullie buys a cure—

For something that he can't endure!

Though keepie-up seems lots of fun—
It's smashing in more ways than one!

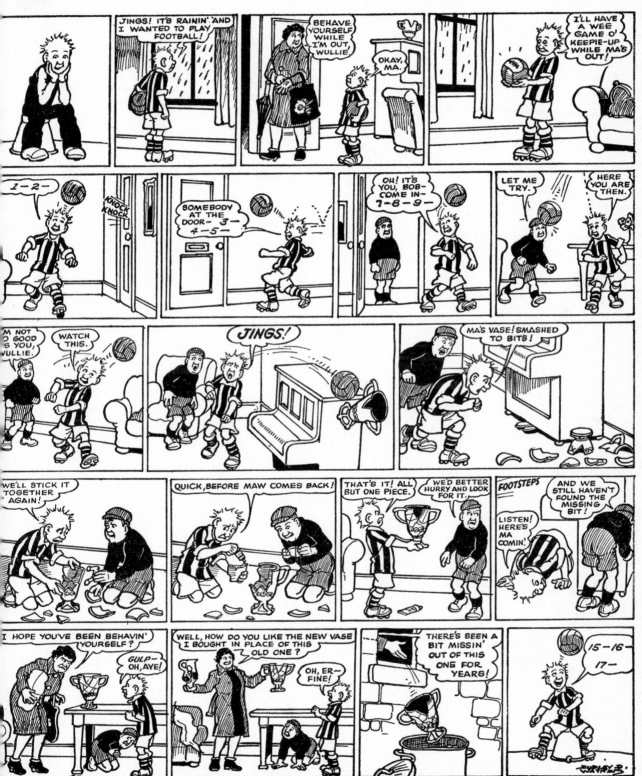

Heap big Injuns on the trail—

Win where all the barbers fail!

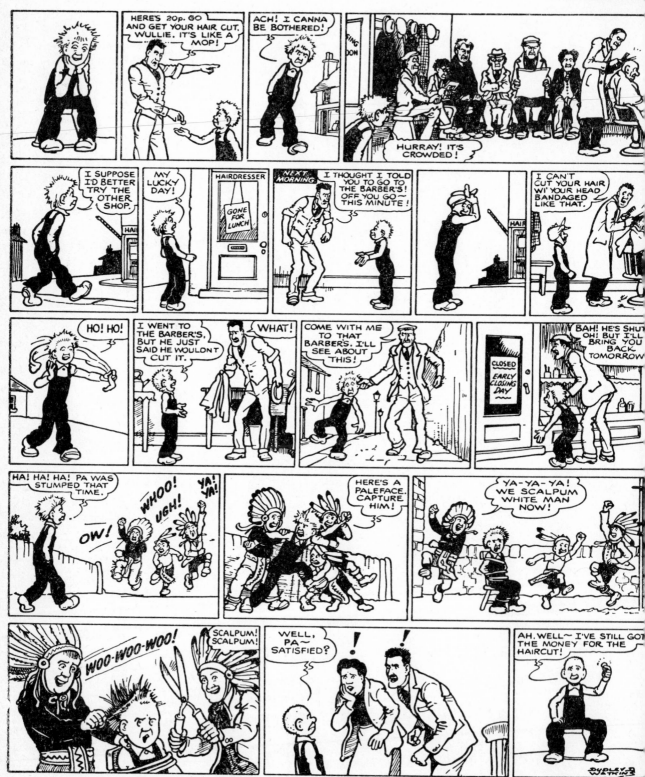

As a fighter, Wull's a smasher—

He fairly dances rings round Basher!

E

For a grandstand seat—

A hod's hard to beat!

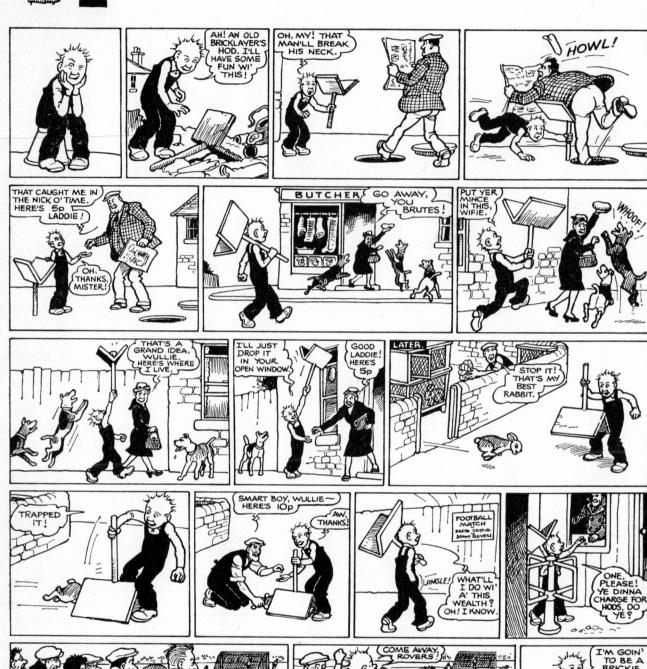

What is this Oor Wullie's got?—

A dog-powered Roman chariot!

See Oor Wullie shake that puss—

He thinks it's gobbled up his moose!

One—two—three flops in a row—

But that bad tooth has got to go!

TWO Oor Wullies? Who is who?—

Trust Ma to know just what to do!

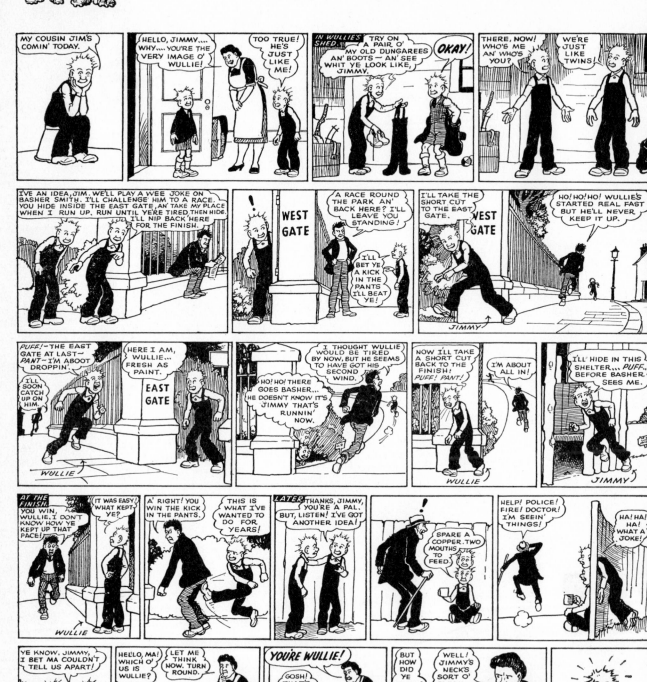

Wullie thinks life sure is tough—

When three mums think that he's too rough!

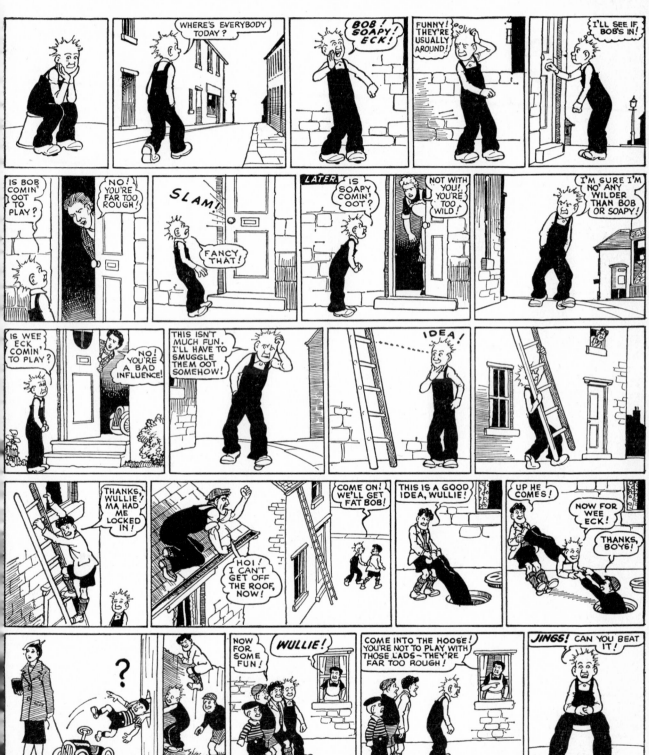

Oor Wullie's happy when there's ice—
But here's one slide that ISN'T nice!

Though 'Wullie' is the name YOU know—

It seems 'twill never be on show!

It's no' half tricky—

Wearin' a dickie!

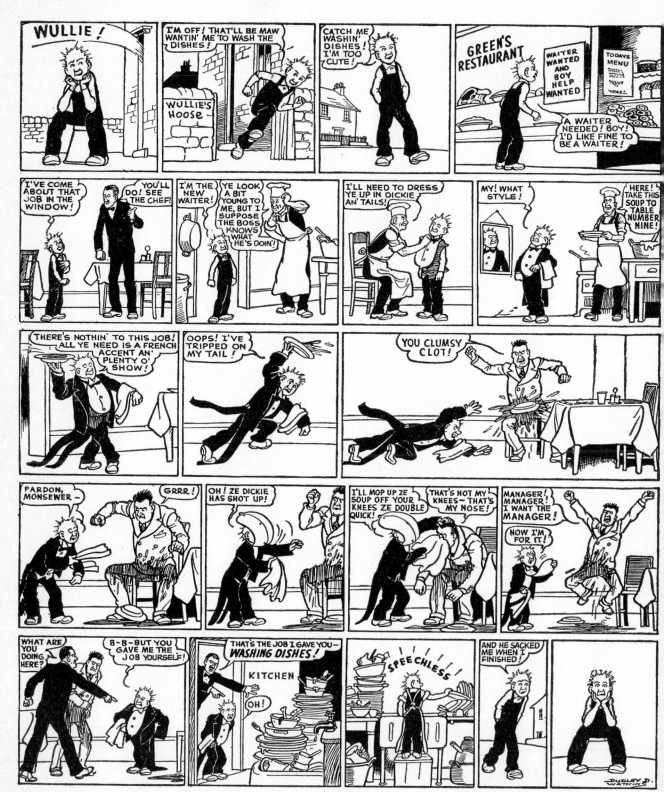

Wullie has no luck today—

It's a real CAT-astrophe!

DON'T BE LATE FOR TEA, WULLIE— IT'S FISH AN' CHIPS!
OH, BOY!

COULD YOU SELL SOME RAFFLE TICKETS FOR ME, WULLIE? IT'S FOR A GOOD CAUSE!

AH! I'LL TRY AND GET THE FISHMONGER TO TAKE A TICKET.
GET OUT O' HERE, YE THIEVIN' WRETCH!

NEVER MIND, MISTER. BUY A TICKET FOR A GOOD CAUSE!

NONE O' YER CHEEK— GET OUT O' THIS!

WHAT DID HE GET MAD FOR?

POOR DICKEY! POOR DICKEY— GONE FOR EVER! THAT NASTY, NASTY CAT!!
NEVER MIND, MISSUS— BUY A TICKET FOR A GOOD CAUSE.

WHY~ YOU~ !!! OF ALL THE CHEEK!

GET OUT OF HERE!

I DON'T KNOW WHAT'S WRONG WITH FOLKS, TODAY— JINGS! LOOK OUT, MISTER!
HOI!

BONK

NEVER MIND, MISTER. BUY A TICKET AND YOU'LL MAYBE WIN A NEW BIKE.
WHAT DOES IT SAY?

YOU MAYBE THINK THAT'S FUNNY, BUT I DON'T!

I CAN'T UNDERSTAND IT. I'LL KNOCK AT THIS DOOR.

BUY A TICKET? I'LL TAKE THE LOT— IT'S FOR A VERY GOOD CAUSE.

YOU'RE A VERY GOOD BOY RAISIN' FUNDS FOR THE LOCAL CAT-LOVERS' SOCIETY.
WHAT?

CAT-LOVERS' SOCIETY! NO WONDER I HAD A JOB SELLING THESE TICKETS!

I'LL GO HOME FOR MY FISH AN' CHIPS.

FISH AN' CHIPS— HERE I COME!

OH-ER— WULLIE!
I'M SORRY, WULLIE, THERE'S ONLY CHIPS— YOU SEE, THE CAT STOLE YOUR FISH!

WHAT I'VE SUFFERED THIS DAY FOR CATS!

He'll never be a millionaire—
But trust oor lad—he won't despair!

Fat Bob's going to get big shocks—

Wullie's 'treasure' walks and talks!

I'M GOIN' TO THE SEASIDE TOMORROW.

SO AM I!

I'LL MAYBE FIND A BOTTLE WI' A MESSAGE IN IT.

—AN' MAYBE THERE'LL BE A MAP.

—AN' THEN I'LL FIND A BURIED TREASURE.

—AN' BE AWFUL RICH!

DON'T BE DAFT!

NEXT DAY
—AN' HE THINKS HE'LL FIND A BOTTLE WI' A MESSAGE IN IT, TELLING HOW TO FIND A BURIED TREASURE!

OH, AYE! WE COULD PUT A FAKE MESSAGE IN A BOTTLE!

LATER HULLO! I'M AWAY TO LOOK FOR A BOTTLE WI' A MESSAGE IN IT.

WELL, THE TIDE'S IN. LOOK IN THE HARBOUR.

TALK ABOOT LUCK! HERE'S A BOTTLE WAITIN' FOR ME.

WHIT A PITY! WE'LL NEED TO GET YE DRIED.

BUT I'VE GOT THE BOTTLE!

LATER HOORAY! THERE'S INSTRUCTIONS INSIDE FOR FINDING BURIED TREASURE. I'M RICH!

IT SAYS, GO TO THE END OF THE HARBOUR BAR—

HARBOUR BAR
SALOON

AH! THAT'S THE HARBOUR BAR. WHAT'S NEXT?

AH! IT SAYS, HEAD FOR THE FISHING SMACKS—

AH! THAT'S IT! A FISH BEING SMACKED!

ACH! HE'S NO' FOLLOWIN' THE INSTRUCTIONS PROPERLY AT ALL!

FISHMONGER

SMACK

I'M GETTIN' ON FINE. IT SAYS NOW, WALK NORTH TILL YOU FIND IT SANDY—

HELLO, SANDY!

HI-YA, JOCK!

AH! THERE'S SANDY!

THEN TURN EAST— 15 PACES AND THE TREASURE IS BELOW YOU.

WULLIE'S GOT IT A' WRONG!

—14—15— IT MUST BE BELOW ME IN THE BURN.

SCREAM!

OH! MY WEE TIMMY!

HOWL!

HE'LL NEVER FIND THE TREASURE I LEFT FOR HIM.

THANK YOU, LADDIE! OH! MY WEE TREASURE!

HERE'S 50p

HE DIDN'T FOLLOW THE DIRECTIONS RIGHT AT ALL! HE WAS SUPPOSED TO FIND THIS!

THESE MESSAGES IN BOTTLES ARE RIGHT ENOUGH!

DUDLEY D. WATKINS

Buns, then nuts and ice-cream, too—

They all go down well at the zoo!

Seaside fun, far inland—

That is what Oor Wullie's planned!

A bully boasts of his good luck—

But Wullie sees him come unstuck!

Oor Wullie finds, to his dismay—

He could have WHEELED this lot away!

Here's a proper laughalot—

'Baby' Wullie in his cot

Oh, what a hoot—

With this 'Royal Salute'!

This trainer hasn't much to do—

There's just ONE casualty—guess who!

Wullie's idea of hiking—

Is not to Dick's liking!

Some surprising—

Hypnotising!

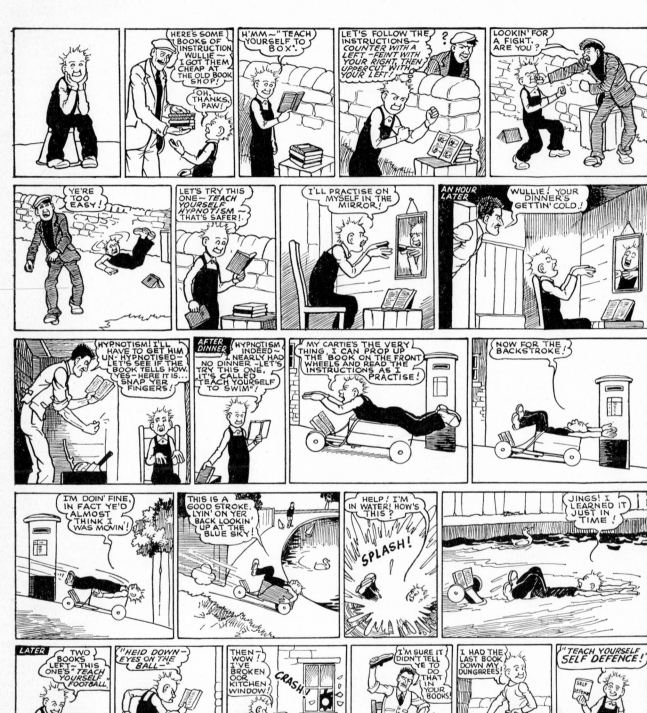

Oh, what a plight—

When he's chasing a kite!

Soppy shoes for Wullie? Never!—

He shows Ma he's far too clever.

There's dismay and gloom—

In the headmaster's room!

An easy job? Not a chance!—
This bird leads Wull a merry dance!

A free feed for Wull's pals—that's good!—
All they have to bring is—food!

Watch oor lad! He's going to find—

It isn't easy being kind!

Wull's trusty blade is made of wood—

But it's sure good for spearing food!

A farmer gets a big shock when—

A sheep goes 'tuck-tuck!' like a hen.

The fun's always hearty—

When HE'S at a party!

An arrow points the way—

To Wullie's Hogmanay

Printed and published by D. C. Thomson & Co., Ltd., 12 Fetter Lane, London E.C.4.
© D. C. Thomson & Co., Ltd., 1974.